The
Heart of
Love

Mary Magdalene Speaks

Gail Swanson

Printing: 5 4 3 2 1   Year 10 09 08 07 06

Printed in the United States of America

Book design and typesetting by Swan Graphics. Cover art by Kate Swanson. Images courtesy of Chant Art at www.holycards.com

A friend for life is
a most magnificent thing.

A sister of the heart is a gift
immeasurable.

Unconditional love is
why we are here.

The merging of heaven and earth
is our divine destiny.

For all this and more . . . this is for you
Sally, my sister, my heart.

To Jesus and Mary Magdalene, my guides,
my strength, my love, my hope.
To Archangel Michael, my companion
and protector throughout all time.
To Saint Joan of Arc, for her faith and courage
and continuous guidance.
To Saint Therese, for showing me the importance and
divinity of her little way and granting me
the understanding of the higher view.
To all The Beloveds who so lovingly communicate
with me every day.
And to my husband Joel, the love of my life, no words can ever
express his contribution in making this book possible.
His belief in all that is unseen and his belief in me has
nourished and supported me. His dedication and loyalty
have inspired me to continue on when I thought I could not.
He has taught me the true meaning of love.
To my mother and father who blessed me with a beautiful beginning.
To my son Erik, whose entrance into this world and my life made me
intensely feel we were not together for the very first time.
His sensitive nature and wisdom beyond his years made me look at
the world and beyond in an expanded way. He is the boy that
opened my eyes and won my heart.
To my daughter Kate, we are one in all things. She is the wisdom
I turn to, the love I draw from. When I look at her I feel I am home.
She is beauty and laughter and all that is magical. I thank my lucky
stars for making this journey with her at my side.

To my 8th grade teacher Sister Grace Maureen, who opened up an incredible new world to me.

To Master Nan Lu, who taught me about energy and oneness and the power within. His kindness and healing meant the world to me during my long illness.

To Dr. Zhao, an angel on earth, who committed himself to solving the mystery of my illness. His presence, love and light is a force of incredible healing.

To Weston Jolly, who sparked my remembering and inspires me to come out and be all I was born to be.

To the shining, magnificent, beautiful Peggy, whose life is a testimony of joy and unconditional love.

To The Jerusalem Girls, Patty, Judy, Barbara and Sally, my divine feminine sisters.

To Garrett, whose light has magnified my world.

To Jaana, whose loving heart and courage continues to inspire me.

And finally to Barbara who demonstrated the same crazy sense of humor as mine from the moment we met. Her humor has so often lifted me, her generosity has graced me and her love has sustained me throughout these many years.

Without each and every one of you this book could never have been possible. I love you and thank you with all of my heart.

Contents

Abbaye de St-André, Lophem (Bruges)   Impr. Heuvelmans, Gand

"As the father has sent me, I am sending you."
And with that he breathed on them and said,
"Receive the Holy Spirit."

John 20:22

Miracles

The Heart of Love

This is a miraculous story. This is a story of angels and saints. It has been given to help us remember that we are not alone. It is being shared to help us remember that what we consider miraculous is right here with us all the time. It has come from on high to encourage us so that we may truly understand that what we seek is within and that what we yearn for is only a breath away.

This is my story and it began on an ordinary day. I had been very sick for many years and I was lying on my bed resting and meditating when the event that changed my life and my world occurred. Suddenly it seemed a wind was being blown into me and the power of it was so strong that my arms repeatedly flew up off the bed. As this was happening I was seeing a vision of Jerusalem. I was seeing pictures but I was also receiving information and the information was about Mary Magdalene. It was about Mary Magdalene and me. When it was over I sat up on the bed and said out loud "They gave me The Breath of The Holy Spirit".

The information I received was so astounding, so completely unbelievable that I told myself I would never be able to tell a soul but the energy of this experience was such that it could not be contained. I was beside myself with excitement, astonishment and confusion and the knowing that something had happened that was so beyond this world that my life would never be the same.

Looking back there were previous signs that something was happening. There were moments and incidents that seemed to be overwhelmingly powerful and moving. My dreams were changing. I seemed to be almost remembering what I was doing at night. I would wake with the essence of having been working in other realms. People began appearing in my life and we would instantly have an exchange that would feel so familiar, as if you had known them your whole life. These meetings would somehow lead me to a new place or a new finding.

I believe the very beginning of this incredible journey began at a little shrine dedicated to St. Michael The Archangel in Tarpon

The Heart of Love

Springs, Florida. This shrine was built because of a little boy who was dying. As the boy lay with no hope of recovery he told his mother that St. Michael The Archangel was appearing to him and that he would be cured. The child was near death and the mother believed that he was hallucinating. The boy then told his mother that Michael wanted her to build a shrine and so to ease the boy's mind the mother agreed. At the appointed day and time the boy sat up and was completely well and as she had promised the mother built the shrine to St. Michael right next to her own home. To this day it is lovingly cared for by that same family and there have been many stories of miraculous healings there ever since.

I had been to this town many times but never knew the shrine existed. A few years ago I met a woman who told me about it and said I must be sure to visit it on my next trip. I was not feeling well and Christmas was upon us. My son and his wife were home from California and my daughter and her fiancé were here. We were all very busy with our last minute shopping and preparations but upon waking the day before Christmas Eve I announced to my husband that I must go to the shrine today and that I wanted the whole family to make the trip. I was sure everyone would say they were too busy but without a word everyone said yes.

When we arrived at the shrine we were amazed to see this beautiful little chapel. It stands in all it's simple magnificence right in the middle of all these little houses. As we walked through the door we were instantly moved by the beauty and feeling there. As in a dream I walked up to the very front of this tiny shrine and became so completely overwhelmed with emotion that I began to cry. I cried and cried and felt as though I could just keep crying forever. My husband looked rather alarmed and asked what was happening but I could not speak. After a while I became calm and just sat there in the quiet of this special place

and wished I could remain there forever. I was not instantly cured of my long illness but something happened to me at the Shrine of St. Michael The Archangel because ever so slowly I began to get better.

The many events that took place from that day on are for another book and another time. What I have been guided to reveal here are the writings that began to emerge. They are as the vision was, from another realm beyond this world. As I sit each morning the words begin to come in stories, prayers and in poetry.

As I struggled to come to terms with how and why Mary Magdalene had come into my life and my writing, she began to appear everywhere. When to my amazement the DaVinci Code came out I decided not to read it. I was already deeply immersed in my morning writing. It was impossible, however, not to see the synchronicity of this event and the many others that were to follow. Mary Magdalene was entering our consciousness, our world and our lives.

I believe that miracles abound. I believe that the angels and saints are always speaking to us and helping us. I believe that we are meant to remember who we are and where we come from and most of all where we are going. I believe that love and truth are the only things that matter and I know that in sharing our stories we have the ability to help to heal one another and the world.

May the loving words that follow enter your hearts and fill you with love, hope and truth and most of all may they help you to remember.

The Heart of Love

Lift me up
oh heavenly father
comfort and console me
oh heavenly mother
teach me how to dance again
in the light of all that is beautiful
lift me up oh angels on high
sing to me the songs of heaven
spread your wings so I may see
kiss me once so I may feel
call me back so I may hear
grant me peace so I may rest
lift me up oh wonders of light
for I am in need of my true home
lift me up beyond the stars
carry and guide me to all that I yearn for
for sometimes here I am lost and frightened
and sometimes here I am ever alone
so lift me up oh my beloveds
lift me up and carry me home

The Heart of Love

All honor and glory is yours
ask and you shall receive
speak and you shall be heard
live in the light of the truth
and walk the path of beauty always
numb yourselves no more
for in allowing yourselves to feel
your hearts will open
and all will flood in
through a beautiful stream
of remembrance
of all that you are
toil not over things you cannot control
and turn your thoughts and intentions
to the way you wish things to be....
for in the wishing can come the believing
and in the believing comes faith
and when faith is truly found
all things are possible

The Heart of Love

Oh it is in the wishing
oh it is in the believing
for this is where magic lives
in the hearts and minds
that have turned to the dreaming
hearts that soar
on the wings of a prayer
minds that are open
to believe the impossible
for wishing and dreaming
create the believing
and the heart of believing
is where miracles are born

Mary Speaks

The Heart of Love

As my name began to emerge through not only the rising of the feminine but through the discovery of the tangible evidence of my life, the world began it's debate in earnest.

Discoveries always cause excitement and varied opinions. And so it shall be... but this my beloveds, is a discovery of the heart... for it is true that all that dwells within my heart and all that I have been, dwells within you. For what matters here is the discovery of what is suppressed in every heart and what is yearned for in every soul.

These truths can only be found within.

As the ways of the world continue to distract and frighten I come forth to ignite the memory of all that you are.

It is true that the strongest of souls shall be drawn to the task of excavating, healing and discovering their own illumination, for then you shall take the hand of another and another and aid in sparking their own true memory.

The power of the natural balance of the masculine and feminine is a power most mighty and a most sacred healing balm.

All that lies beneath the destruction of this most natural state is beautiful and born of heaven.

How shall the balance be restored?

When the divine feminine connects to the stars and heaven and breathes the remembrance into her physical body on earth, this shall create a power reborn.

13

The Heart of Love

When the masculine connects in this way, igniting his own divine feminine and heavenly qualities, he may then acknowledge this sweetness and grace with loving acceptance and one shall see the sweetness in another and another.

In the living sanctuary of your heart, all that has been suppressed, all that has been wounded, all that cries out for love, is now ready to be uncovered and released.

I understand your feeling that the process is never ending but this I am afraid is the process upon the earth.

Your choice to be the shining stars in the face of such anguish illuminates in ways you shall never know.

Allow yourselves to open now in ways you have not allowed for in this allowance fear shall be shattered and love and peace shall reign.

And as you embrace these ancient ways and call out the names of all who adore you the luminous fibers of your heavenly being shall illuminate and connect with your heavenly home.

Continue to call upon the memory of love.

Hold fast in your desire for truth.

Seek only the truth within.

For there you shall find....your own sacred heart.

The Heart of Love

Cast all doubts
all fears
and all inadequacies
to the wind
for the breath of the holy spirit rides upon the wind
and as she imbues you with the power
to acknowledge the divinity within
so does she carry all burdens upon her wings
and with her breath
releases all unto the wind

see and feel her descend upon you
acknowledge the enlightenment filling your hearts
release to her all of the heaviness
thanking her for her majesty and grace

breathe now
as we begin to remember

breathe now
into your spirit

allowing the heaviness
of the body
to fall

and feel your connection
to your own true spirit

The Heart of Love

feel your connection
to one another

feel your connection
to all that is

breathe now beloveds
and let us begin

let us begin
the journey back home

The Breath

The Heart of Love

Beneath the dark illusion
a light is shining there
beneath the broken hearted
love is beating still
and through the blackest nights
of earthly disappointment
the breath of all that's holy
fills us and sustains us
reminds us of the stillness
and peace that dwells within
for living in the light of peace
we offer to the world
the sacred and the blessed
the breath of all that's true
the magic of our heart's intent
a gift of love transcending
the breath of sweet remembrance
of how the world should be
just one united breath of all
one powerful breath of love

The Heart of Love

This is a message
that comes from on high
breathe as you read
for you will remember
who you are
and why you have come
beauty and strength
and infinite love
all these things
of which you are made

heavenly forces surround you
and guide you
sparking your memories
and gently awakening
your soul's remembrance
of heaven's sweet sounds

all of the majesty
all of the splendor
is yours to receive
if you open your heart
breathe in and feel
your eternal divinity
for it shines within
and is calling you home

The Heart of Love

Lift yourselves up... up
out of this dense world
feel your soul soar and fly
know your spirit is free
and is always working
outside the vehicle
of your physical body

acknowledge your flight
know you are of the stars
and of heaven

hear us whisper your name

we call you back
we urge you to remember

we are here
do you feel us?

know that the essence of you
is most powerful
and serves a magnificent purpose

how to integrate the two
the physical and the spirit
it is found in the quiet of the breath
it is your truest nature
and your most heavenly right

The Heart of Love

fly with us
call to us
as we call to you

it is easier than you perceive

all wonders are yours
for the time is now
and we receive you with open arms

may you silence your mind
and open your heart
may you soar with the angels
and may you breathe
and remember home

The Heart of Love

Let us speak now of the connection of the breath
and the voice
be ever conscious of it
for if you are conscious of the breath in relationship
to the voice
you will begin to experience a new way of speaking

speaking from the heart, without effort, without thought
for the breath and the intention of honoring the breath
will lead you to speak from your heart and your soul

yes, soul speaking

the breath will help to bypass the busy mind
telling you what to say, and what not to say
and if you use the voice
and understand this most precious gift of breath and voice
you will truly begin to speak in divine connection with heaven

you will feel transformed

and you will transform those to whom you speak

take a deep breath with pure intention before you speak
and as you are speaking

this is the universal divine connection
you will remember....
and you will live with a conscious connection

The Heart of Love

to the breath of the holy spirit
and the voice will come forth
powered by this sacred connection
and you will begin to speak

using the voice

honoring the voice

and in every moment
you will create a vibration
that will change the world

The Heart of Love

What does it mean for you to be free?
how would it feel to say I am free?
few on earth have lived in true freedom
for the things of the world distract and diminish

in situations of conflict and wars of destruction
you allow yourselves to consider freedom
freedom of speech, freedom from oppression
laws you have made and concepts you believe in
but what of within?

may you truly see where conflict and shackles that bind lie
they are created in the mind and live in the body
and slowly rob you
of remembering how it feels to be free
to breathe each breath fully and completely
without fear or anxiety
to breathe each breath as manna from heaven
for in the acknowledgment of the breath of freedom
you will open to the origin of the breath

breathe now with full intention
breathe now with the understanding
of the act of breathing
for it is with the first breath you shall live
and with the last breath you shall die

the breath is the connection to the divine
and the secret to unlocking the truth that dwells within

Messages
for the
Divine Feminine

The Heart of Love

Hearts unite
blessed in love
carry light from above
sing the song
meant to sing
open hearts showering
golden light reflecting all
holy women hear the call
we remember we will see
all that we are meant to be
graceful beauty guiding beam
we awaken to the dream

The Heart of Love

Let down your guard
oh women of heaven
let all fall away
as you gather in love
for none of these things
shall hinder or bind you
as you choose to live
in the light of the truth
speak from your soul now
all that you must
look in these faces
and see your own
do not separate
or draw back your beauty
for here are your sisters
and they know who you are
you may rest now
in the arms of the angels
and begin to feel
your true shining purpose
heaven applauds you
and lifts you ever higher
think now of nothing
but the calling of home

The Heart of Love

Women of my heart
blessed are you for all that you are
life springs forth from your wombs
and all is made new again and again
the love and hope of the ages flows through you
and touches all with beauty and grace
do not forget the power that is yours
the energy of the moon so soft and brilliant

the time has come
awake from your slumber

if you ask all will be given
all must fall away
and balance must be restored
a new day is dawning and you hold the key
to peace and infinite love

cast all doubt to the wind
close your eyes and breathe
for the strength and remembrance
is as soft as a whisper and as powerful as the sea
capture it
feel it
remember
for I am with you
and bring you great truths
fear not for all is about to manifest
gather as we once did and call to heaven
we rejoice at you're choosing
to remember who you are

The Heart of Love

Guiding lights
beacons of hope and strength
women of passion and power
create the world as you dream it
look within
beyond the worries
and anxieties of the world
quiet yourselves
and feel
all that you are
stand in your beauty
bring forth the memory of your soul's purpose
magnify your worth
for it is beyond what you perceive
sanctify the holiness of your feminine nature
call down the moon
and breathe in the sun
for you are the power and brilliance
of all of these wonders

The Heart of Love

As women we bring forth a great vibration
we are one with the energy of the earth
and within us lies the radiance and power of the moon
the moon is our sister
she rises sweetly and when all is quiet
and bathes the world with a delicate and nurturing light
there are those of you who have awakened to her embrace
and connection to her
spend time with her
feel her energy resonate within you
draw her in with the breath
with complete intention
there is much she will give you
as you acknowledge her

yes, we are the women of the moon and the sea
we are radiant and fluid
ever steady and ever moving
we are the mystery and the power
we are the wisdom of the ages
we are here now to raise the consciousness of mankind
we turn with the tides and welcome the change
for we have waited long
and are bursting with truth and love
we will grow in number
raising our voices
as they reach the heavens and shifts are created
from the sheer power of our feminine vibration

The Heart of Love

come together and sing
for you will remember
the song of your birth
and you will remember your sisters
each and every one

the separation created by man
will no longer serve
as in unity
like so many who have come before

we glorify and sanctify
and bless ourselves and one another

in the name of those who walked the earth
in the most holy divinity
we bow our heads and say

yes

The Heart of Love

On a dark and starry night
as I stand beneath the moon
I bathe in the light
as I feel her soft embrace
when the moon calls my name
and the world is ever still
my soul begins to sigh
and I remember who I am

The Heart of Love

Shall we speak of what remains hidden?
will you reclaim your rightful place?
for all lies before you and the time is at hand
and this gathering is the proclamation
will you proclaim what you know to be true?
will you not deaden these stirrings within?
for they shall continue to stir and disrupt
they shall continue to call in the night
when did the pushing under begin?
long ago
for much has caused you to fear speaking
and fear being known
but known you are and so divinely supported
for the truth is vibrating and shall not be quieted
not by man nor situation
not by falsehoods so cleverly employed
the day dawns for the women awaken
the heavens sing for this power united
do not cry nor suffer in silence
for the scales fall away and the voices are found
hold hands and unite your voices
feel the memory of love's vibration
for love is the touch of your sister's hand
and love is the sound of a voice raised freely
may you drop each hidden agenda
may you flow in this love created
hands, hearts and voices
pathways to remembrance
circle of sisters finding their way home

The Heart of Love

The women are gathering, yes, and the power will
be restored when the feminine takes her rightful place once
again. Do not think this is not coming, for it is to be.
The feminine strength that you posses will be magnified,
electrified, till all ears will hear and all eyes will see. And
the heavens will rejoice as the prophecy is fulfilled and the
bride is returned to her place with her beloved.

It is here, it is now. It has been foretold.
The energy of the new day propels you forward into the
restructuring of all life on earth. As this begins to take
place, heavens doors will open and the rejoicing will be
heard throughout every dimension for the loss of the
feminine has been the devastation of this planet. Think
nothing less for this is the root of all darkness. The light
of the feminine is returned in the vehicle of Mary
Magdalene and all women.

This power will grow in strength and beauty until
all is changed and made new again, as it was in the
beginning, balance restored. The dominion of the
masculine over the feminine will no longer be. Your eyes
are opening and you shall see things you never dreamed.

Rest in the knowing that you have done well and all
is unfolding in a most sacred manner.

Each of you are here not by accident but by divine providence. Each of you have had the stirrings of these things which we will now speak. Male or female the issue at hand is the divine feminine within us all. Do you understand the magnitude of this powerful energy being suppressed? This suppression over the ages has caused energetic eruptions of all kinds. The world as you know it is out of balance. The time is at hand for the feminine to come back into balance, and yes, we must hasten with our awakening to all this means.

The energetic power of women gathering in truth can be likened to breaking the sound barrier, a boom shaking and resonating in every dimension. Powerful divine forces contained in physical bodies, thoughts and emotions and deep inner knowings growing stronger and stronger. May we speak of these things for this is the issue and you hold in your hands the divine prescription of love that will change the world.

Women of the heart drop the sorrow and anger of the past and move sweetly forward for the new day is most assuredly dawning and you have been called to assume your rightful place, a place that is most honored and blessed.

This you know, this you feel, though much has been done to push you into a realm of forgetting. Do not fear, for the forgetting is false and has come to an end. Are you aware of how the sacred feminine has been denied, pushed aside and driven under? Oh yes, for you have lived it many times over and carry the pain and struggle.

As you breathe in the remembrance of who you truly are, you will speak these truths and say no more will I be quiet, no more will I

settle for that which does not serve me nor the world nor the universe. I stand in my divinity, tall, beautiful and proud and sing the beautiful song of my birth so that all may hear it's magnificent vibration and remember.

Magnify and sanctify. Open to a whole new world of possibilities. Cast off the shackles of the past. Revel in the glory of the new day. Find within yourselves the memory of love that you have convincingly buried for it is there as sure as the stars shine. This love shines ever so brightly within. Hearts laden with grief and despair and such loneliness, hearts longing to remember but layered with hurts that began the forgetting. Why must you hold on?

These manifestations of betrayal and pain are merely re-enactments of the one we hold most dear. His message has always been of love and deep abiding honor for that which is the feminine. He walked in beauty on this earth with full divine knowledge of all that reigns within. We are no different. We hold the divine seeds of remembrance in our hearts and are meant to live in the light of the Resurrection.

If you allow yourselves the release of all that is designed to hold you back you will experience the transcendence of self and move to a level of understanding that will make your heart sing.

This is for you, for each of you, for you are most holy and most divine and carry the vibration that was created to give the world a most magnificent gift, that which a mother gives to her child, the gift of unconditional love. Hold this feeling and memory in your heart center and bring it out to radiate to all the world. For we are one and all hold within the key to peace on earth and love that knows no bounds.

The Heart of Love

Flowering and growing
bursting forth with color and radiance
each one of you concentrating on your own opening
and coming forth
we wish you to know it does not go unnoticed
we wish you to know how very much
it matters in your world
such positive energies emerging and vibrating
understand that this way of living
has the power to change anything
and this it does
what you consider miraculous becomes commonplace
when hearts are truly open and you are not afraid to see
but you must be ever vigilant
and not fall into the act of complacency
this seemingly harmless state is one of inertia
and will halt the forward motion
this is not meant to say that you may not rest
for you may always rest and are encouraged to do so
what we speak of now is what you already understand
just be aware that when it becomes more comfortable
to turn away from yourself
it would be wise
not to linger

The Heart of Love

I have chosen to stand in my power
I have chosen to speak out and sing
the song of my birth
the song of my destiny
the song that connects me
to every living thing
I am awakening
I am emerging
powerful woman
as strong as the sea
see me shining
see me most radiant
for I have chosen
to remember and be
powerful and glorious
knowing and compassionate
woman reborn
in my choice to be free

Memories of
the Beloved

The Heart of Love

Listen to the soft whispers
as your heart begins to speak
in divine union with heaven
open to how it feels
to be unafraid of worlds unseen
watch as all are transfixed and transformed
by this soulful exchange of heart and heaven
understand the power in this place
let yourself pause and integrate this majesty
for you have come far and we have been waiting
all will unfold beyond your imagination
all is made ready for the beautiful ones
all of time melding together
all of space so infinite and vast
spiritual beings in all dimensions
join together in the beautiful dance

The Heart of Love

If only you could hear the sound of his voice
or know his touch

these things I wish for you all

but oh the beauty of your faith in feeling him in your heart
you must understand that knowing him in this way
is so honored and blessed
for it is faith that has the power to move mountains

I speak of him with utmost devotion and love
for it was he that showed me the divinity that reigned within
and this is what I wish to share with you
for the time is at hand
and it is just and right that you should revel in the knowing
of your most beautiful and divine hearts

he came to show us not only who he was
but who we are

this is the message

in recognizing and understanding the truth
we are able to see the truth in ourselves
let us go forth
no longer thinking
this divinity exists external to ourselves

see the beauty in another
and you shall see it in yourself
let yourselves open to feel it all
love, compassion, sorrow and pain
and the joy and ecstasy of feeling
the radiant soul you truly are

The Heart of Love

Walking with him
talking with him
looking at him
caring for him
being completely
mesmerized by him
the way he looked
the way he spoke
the way he walked

you would just drink him in

all else paled in comparison

if he was out of your sight
you could still feel him
but your eyes would grieve
for he is all they wished to see

living became like a dream
with harsh interruptions of reality

rumblings about him

the outrage

you could feel the fear

it was palpable

The Heart of Love

this would temporarily wrench you
out of his heavenly world
and the reality would hit
that this would not last
this could not last
this heaven on earth
then his voice and his words would draw you back in
and all would be well and all would be safe

it was strange how there was no fear for self at all
all worry was for him
all normal feelings for one's self just vanished

he was your whole world
and all that mattered
having him in the midst of the harsh light of day
in a world full of suffering and atrocities

he was the sacred balm
he was the living testament of love
he was the dearest one

to be divinely transcended as he was on earth
to be in that presence
to feel it so completely
it was transcending for us
for all who had the ability to see the truth
of who he was

The Heart of Love

the others
they allowed fear to overtake them
we chose love
they chose fear

we chose truth
they chose lies

but the transcendence of all who walked with him
is still being felt
and it will grow stronger
allow yourselves to feel it now
for if you are hearing these words
of truth and infinite love
then you may feel....

open your hearts
dispel all doubt and fear and judgment

feel the love of the most beloved enter your hearts
and live as we did then

for he is surely with you
 as he was then

and through these words
beckons you

to feel

and remember

The Heart of Love

His eyes were blue. The kind of blue you just get lost in. His hands were most gentle and his voice seemed to come from another place for it went completely into you and filled you. He was firm in his words but ever so loving. The love that was emanating from him either captured you or turned you away. There were those that could not handle his presence. He worried as we did, but not of the small as we do. His worries were for mankind, he so wanted all to hear the message of love and the love in his heart was not of this world. He was bringing heaven to us, through his eyes, his touch and his voice.

If there had been no miracles his presence would have been enough but he so wanted to touch even those who could not believe. So he made manifest the wonders, but that is not what he was about. It was simple really. It was meant to change the minds and hearts and turn them towards love and forgiveness. Imagine bringing a message of such magnitude, knowing what the end would be.

And yet he did these things with great beauty and care. He was happy to do it. He was full of joy, which is something you never hear about. He was very lighthearted and laughed easily and often. He could be easily annoyed as well for the bickering and pettiness was something he had not much patience for but always he forgave it. And this is what he taught. He taught this at a time when much of it angered those who were ingrained in their beliefs and positions for the way he loved the women was not understood and infuriated many. He came to say we are all one and this is the way he lived. The women just adored him. They were lifted up on high and could feel the truth. He helped them remember who they were.

The Heart of Love

Now we must speak of today. How will we bring his message back into the hearts of those who still run from him? It is in this place and time that the opportunity for great change exists. There are things taking place of which you are not aware, shifts and energies coming forth to facilitate peace and love and a great light if only you will choose.

I am happy to be heard in this time and place. Some will be angered, for as it was then, the message is strong and the vibration it carries frightens those who are layered with guilt and shame. This is unnecessary for the time has come to lift your faces and see the beauty, for he is still with you.

He is with you in one and other and more and more of you are choosing love and speaking of this love, for love begins with the truth and the truth has been hidden. Do you understand what we are speaking of? Yes, that love is the answer, for he was the embodiment of all that is loving and demonstrated this love for all, for the women, the children and those who would do away with him. Forgiveness, truth, faith, integrity, I say again, it is simple.

He gave us the feeling of oneness, the feeling of being in balance with ourselves, one another and the universe. In thinking they could end the message by doing away with his physical body they were denying all that is real and all that is true. And as men do, they were carried away by their egos and the lies they tell themselves, and jealousy and position reigned but the women were transformed and the women understood. And so they taught and so they spoke and their words were killed by men as they killed him. But as he lived on without his physical body, so did the message, in all it's majesty, through the hearts and souls of the women who loved him.

And today, in this time and place, the rumblings of truth will turn to a thunderous roar and the balance will be restored, for the denial of the woman, of the feminine, has caused great destruction and unhappiness. Open your hearts to receive all you know to be true. Walk with him once again for the message is within you. He has placed it there within your heart and all that needs be done is to allow yourselves to open and remember.

The Heart of Love

He so loved the water, to walk by it, to gaze at it and to bathe in it. The water is the symbol on earth of cleansing and renewal. The water, the symbol of rebirth. He felt of the water, it soothed and comforted him. Many days he would choose to speak at the waters edge to allow all to feel this comfort and beauty as he spoke.

They were silent as he spoke and then at times they would call out to him and ask him to explain. He was mostly so patient with these inquiries but there were times when he would seem angered and would answer them strongly.

He was aware of what was needed, yes, but he wearied at times at what felt like such an enormous task. He worried, was he accomplishing it at all?

But, and this I can never truly explain, what transpired when he would speak. It would be as if an invisible force would just envelop you and the whole world would fall away and you knew, you absolutely knew you were hearing and participating in something not of this world. Oh yes, you could feel it, it was palpable. You were unaware of the crowd, the heat, your life, anything. And you must understand we were used to prophesizing. This was, as I said, it cannot be explained.

I felt this way from the moment I saw him and ever more did this grace remain upon me and within me for I was forever transformed and forever grateful for one such as he to look upon me and know me and tenderly receive me. So powerful was this that no earthly thing could take you from it, not for me. This is what he gave me, brought to earth from heaven with such love and devotion!

The Heart of Love

From the moment I saw him I was unable to cry for myself, all tears were for him, such was the magnitude of my love for him. It was unthinkable, what he came to do, and he was a man, a most beautiful man. And in honor and truth I tell you, he felt for me in this way, and so we lived and so we loved in a way that had never been. And the secret that lies within my heart is divine and infinite. May all who hear these words share with me, the memory and love of the most beloved one.

The Heart of Love

There was a woman who came to him in great distress
but afraid to tell him of her true plight
for she was mistreated and not shown love
and she lived in despair and utter loneliness

so he told her of the love that was all around her
the love of the birds and the love of the trees

he taught her to breathe in the light of heaven
and he touched her and glorified her with his infinite love

he told her of the light that dwells within
the one that was hidden by those who lived in darkness

he told her to find it and let none take this from her
for she was so beautiful and worthy of such a gift
and no matter her circumstance she was now lifted
for he touched in her the remembrance of love
for she had forgotten as none had shown her
but now she remembered the love within

for in his eyes she saw her own
and in his heart she felt pure love
and on this day she lifted her face
and on this day she received his blessing
and all was made new and all was made right
for she could now feel the light of heaven
shining upon her with its infinite grace

The Heart of Love

this is the way he touched them and healed them
this was the beauty he extended to all

his radiant heart enveloping the sorrowful
his loving hands healing hearts and bodies

this he gave to all who came to him
this heaven he brought for us here on earth
in this same way he is still with you
in this same way does he still touch your heart
open your eyes and receive this remembrance
open your hearts and remember love

There was a day
it was quite close feeling and hot
and he wished to escape the burden of the crowds
his need for the water always so great
his love of all nature so blessed and holy
so once again he would escape to the water
and once again it would refresh and renew
and there would he leave all his worries and anguish
and there would he be
at one with the sea

The Heart of Love

Oftentimes a sadness would come upon him
and he would feel overwhelmed
by all he was sent to do
he wants you to know that because of this
he understands
all the human emotions
he was not exempt from feeling these things
but he would pray and ask for guidance and help
and his faith that all was as it should be
would help him continue

he spoke of many things
he spoke about free will and free choice
the simplicity of it
the beauty of it
he spoke of the darkness that invaded people's beings
and how he felt for them

he spoke of love
how love truly is the answer to all

a closed heart, a broken heart, a bitter heart
these heartfelt emotions leading people's lives

in opening to receive love
all negative feelings of the heart
are washed away
and as each heart is changed
from pain, hurt and anger
to joy and love

The Heart of Love

then this change
will be passed on
to the next and yet the next

this is the only way
a kind word or touch is all it takes
when a hardened heart is made soft
a kindness may then come forth
and oh the meaning of this kindness
to one who has been trained not to expect it

this was what he spoke of in quiet moments

The Heart of Love

He spoke with us as we stood by his side. He told us not of himself but of ourselves. He spoke of our gentleness and beauty, he spoke of the comfort we gave. He taught us ways to connect with our power. He led us to discover our divinity. He felt the plight of the woman was as his plight, for women possessed such knowledge and power but lived in a world where it could not be expressed. More than this they would be punished and outcast, more than this they would be spat upon and stoned.

For this he came to encourage us and open us, to understand that it mattered not, these ways of the world designed by men, these ways of the world, abusing their power. He gave us the strength to work as he did, for he told us we possessed the same light as he.

In many ways he felt as we did, knowing that speaking would bring him great harm. He did not want us to suffer in this way, he deflected all unto himself, and ever quietly did he have us working and ever purposefully did he have us reveal, all things heavenly and all things loving for when with him we cared not of this world.

So we walked with him and we watched as he spoke and we sat with him and we were touched as he healed and our power rose within our physical bodies, and our love grew more than we had ever known. And as women we transcended all time and space, as we danced with him, the dance of divine love.

The Heart of Love

Healing hands
healing words
healing touch
living
breathing
knowing
walking in truth
blessing all around him
lifting them
caring for each precious soul
as if it were the one and only
pulling them higher with words and acts
that would raise them out of their lives
their thinking
their ignorance
imbuing them with love and knowledge and strength
giving hope and spiritual encouragement
and as those were raised and made dizzy
by this incredible experience
the others used it to fuel and fortify anger and jealousy
and denial of truth
these were the powerful extremes that came together
to create the environment that led to his death
understand the power in your lives in receiving his message
understand what comes from hatred, denial and jealousy
feel in your hearts the true remembrance of love

Mary and Her
Beloved Son

The Heart of Love

Her hands were always diligently working, preparing the food, mending, but much else was done with such hands for always was she healing with those most loving hands. Her voice was soft and so unassuming but never shy when expressing her opinion. There was a glow about her. She shined from within. Many graces could be obtained from just being in her presence for she exuded wisdom, love and vast knowings.

Her love for her family and those dear to her was surpassed by none. The cross she was born to bear existed each day as she struggled to stay in the present for the worry of what was to come could overtake her. Do not think she did not suffer in this way beforehand, for she did, for she was acutely aware of all.

She was in constant prayer. She relished every moment that her eyes were blessed with the sight of her beloved son and she agonized when her eyes were not upon him. And when they were together, walking, talking, laughing, their light would be as one for never could there be a love so precious, so mutual, so glorious! They were, I laughingly shall say, a match made in heaven.

They argued and bantered about, for her advisements were always about his safety and he knew he must do what he must. She spoke her mind as his mother for this she was through and through. And the love she gave him sustained him through all, and the pain that she carried for him eased him and lifted him.

They continue to be the ever present loving energy of mother and child. They exist within and magnify this love for all who turn to

them for comfort and help. They continue to adore these loving relationships and continue to work in unison showering their loving energies upon all.

There is much to be said that has been speculated upon about our beloved mother, mother of all. So much did she teach her own beloved son, so instrumental was she to him for he turned to her for so much.

This loving union set the stage for our loving union and I was ever grateful to her for her love for her son and for me, for the two became three and our trinity was born so the prophecy would be fulfilled. Much was done by this most divine trinity. When merging our energies a power was created and the strength of this was magical.

Think of these things my beloved ones, feel in your hearts these most loving and most heavenly unions. Create in your lives, no matter the trials, the beauty of love, for the mother of heaven and the son of mankind offer this to you with arms open wide.

Mary Consoles

The Heart of Love

Every mother
that carries the agony
of losing a child
is held in the arms
of the most beloved mother

every tear that is shed in sorrow
every cry that is uttered in pain
every prayer that is whispered in silence
every scream unleashed in desperation

all is felt
all is heard
all is honored
in ways you shall never know

where there is no consolation
she consoles
where there is no ray of hope
she shines her light
when life loses all meaning
she bestows the miraculous

she is ever present
and all loving
she heals and soothes
and walks beside you

The Heart of Love

take the hand
of our beloved mother
the hand that caressed
her own fallen son

for at last she reigns
in the heavens
beside him
and this shall be true
for you and for yours

The Beloveds

The Heart of Love

He had a way of placing his hands on either side of my head, so gently, and with such love. And he would look into my eyes and I tell you the world would stop. In this way we were in another world all the time. I drew great comfort in knowing I helped to take him away from it all in these precious moments.

He was always joking for he knew he could always make me laugh and he found my seriousness in certain matters quite amusing. We had an easy flow of seriousness and humor and we had the gift of lifting each other up at just the right moments.

We were, I would have to say, the perfect balance, and this is the balance of which I am speaking. This was the symbol of masculine and feminine in all it's divinity, deep abiding respect and great joy and a love that remains throughout all eternity.

This is available to all who are willing to open their hearts. In opening, especially to his energy, and most important, opening to the feminine energy, you will feel this kind of love and remember at the deepest soul level, that this is the truth, this is the way and this is most assuredly the light.

For the light of love is electrified and magnified when one is touched and seen by their beloved. May you open your hearts to the beauty of this remembrance.

On the days when he was not speaking and when he would be in need of solitude, we would wander away and he would ask to be alone, except for me. This is where the upset was felt. "Why will he take her, a woman and not us? Of course he cannot speak of things in time alone with her, he would only choose us and yet he allows her to come in his private moments."

They felt confusion over this and they allowed this to take over their thinking. It caused them worry, jealousy and all things that cause the mind to stir. It was unfortunate, but they were unable to open completely to the fullness of his truly embracing all. They were meant to struggle, to show themselves certain things and I was meant to speak to them in ways that shocked and provoked, to jar them into knowing that a woman could not only grasp but illuminate all he was saying, for they had deep trouble understanding his words.

If they had allowed themselves to feel more with their hearts, but they were obsessed with dissecting all he had to say, saying "What can he mean by this?" It was understood and felt so deeply, there was no need for words really.

He spoke with his eyes and taught with his touch but they could not see and they could not feel. This is not to say that they did not receive, for they did, and oh how they loved him. This they felt, through and through. His message was always the same, no matter how many ways he attempted to honor them with each story. Yes, they were lifted up on high in the moment and could surely feel heaven through him but always there would be the questioning and the desire to understand in ways that were impossible for them.

I do not mean to say that I was in a unique position but in the sense that I was so honored to be with him in the quiet, this was so. But many of the women were as I was, not needing extra explanation. They were content in the knowing that they did understand and this was good enough, more than good enough.

This is why he loved the women so, for they did not drain him, but nurtured him and fortified him.

If you look at what has now been uncovered, as to what I would ask of him, you will clearly see, for I did not ask for a re explanation of what had been said but would want to know of the spiritual nature and esoteric, for my mind and body did not feel of this world and would exist in realms that were quite heavenly.

It would feel as though my feet were not planted on the ground and my mind was no longer thinking of the worldly but of the other world, the one he was attempting to show us. I felt this.

My connection to him was complete in every way. I do understand this was some sort of advantage and as such we were always communicating in ways that needed no words. There were things I would be given all on my own and there were things he would speak of, because the vibration of his voice was the powerful transcendence.

If you were to only hear the words, not understanding the meaning of one word, a shift would take place for it was meant to go straight to the heart, bypass the mind, and this it did.

Only when they allowed the mind to take them over again and again did they take themselves out of this beautiful experience. These things are imprinted on each soul and in the same way I was lifted and glimpsed this heavenly world and it's majesty, you too have this ability.

For he is ever present.

He is ever with you.

It is the same really, just letting your heart lead the way, bypassing the busy questioning mind. This is accomplished by meditation, prayer and asking for heavenly guidance and support. All will be given if you let yourselves hear with your heart for the heartbeat is the sound of the soul and the voice is the vibration of truth, the eyes, the beams of love.

And this is as was meant to be.

The Heart of Love

What can be said about a love that transcends everything you ever dreamed? What can you say about a love of the purest hearts, energies united in the highest order of love, opening energy centers that created worlds of ecstasy and feelings of such intensity. This could be achieved by just being in his presence. For in the presence of one who illuminates and radiates such overwhelming openness and love, you are lifted to places that did not exist before.

You would become as if transfixed, in a state of complete understanding. This is as it was for me and for many others. For me, however, I lived in a place all the time where this feeling of joy, love and ecstasy was returned by him. If this had not been so I would have suffered unbearably for I knew always that he was to be mine in this way. It was and is a sacred and blessed union. How sweetly and completely he loved, giving all. We were as one, united in love everlasting. We communicated our thoughts without need for words.

It was as simple as breathing.

I was a great comfort to him, and he to me. We were in a world all our own and yet we did everything we were destined to do. There was such love among us all and yet the human minds would still ramble and question and taunt, so there was great restlessness in the minds of many who followed him.

My thoughts were not of these things for somehow I understood all.

The Heart of Love

This is one of the ways in which he was comforted greatly for he could be at rest with me, rest in the knowing that our hearts and minds were one and the love and the teachings were imparted to me with every breath I would take. My awareness of these things was a divine gift for us both.

We never spoke of these things for it was understood and so for this reason he was able to speak in a way he would not to the others for much of what he said went over their heads and they were constantly questioning the meaning of this and that.

It is not to say that I did not question, but it was not in that way. It was always to have an even higher understanding of what was spoken. This higher place is what helped us to bear all that was to come for we could go there in our hearts.

I must admit this did not help when things became so bad for nothing could stop my heart from breaking.

And let it be said and let it be known that his heart was breaking during these times, but not for himself, but for those of us who loved him and those of his enemies.

If only I could explain to you the compassion he felt for all.
It was the most beautiful thing.
This is what lifted him above the rest.
How beautifully he lived. How beautifully he died.

The Heart of Love

We were walking
we were holding hands
he helped me up an incline
and we were looking out across an expanse
he was telling me that he had come to right the wrongs
to open eyes
he said my role was the same
he said I would be remembered throughout time
that my name would be spoken
that I was the symbol of beauty and strength
courage and unity

I would inspire, as he inspired
and one day our names would be spoken together
side by side
as was meant to be
and one day my teachings would be reborn

he said, Mary, you are shining and golden
you hold the keys to the truths of the universe
heaven and earth shall merge
as once again
you will open their hearts
with your words and your heart
speak Mary
for the sound of your voice
is the resonance of heaven itself

The Love of His Life

The Heart of Love

Here she stood by his side
here she was to him
what he was to her
divine and beautiful
comforting and pure

two beloveds cast in a role
beyond human capacity
for completely understanding this

but together they would touch heaven
and together they were as one
united in divinity
united in divine love

she saw him as no one else could
he saw her as no one else would

and in their world most divine
they carried out their heavenly vow
amidst the cruelty of the blinding world
they rose above and walked in the light

for the light of love is all there is
and this he was given to show him and sustain him
for her love filled him as manna from heaven
and her hands held him and softened the blows
for he suffered the injustice of all humanity
and her light was needed to remind him of home

81

The Heart of Love

let us understand
that of all the injustice
what was done to her
when he left this world
was done unto him

for his true message
the one of divine love

the love of two
most holy and sacred

was taken and lost

and ever more
has the world been searching

for the love of the feminine

the love of his life

The Last Days

The Heart of Love

As the time approached and he knew the end was upon him, his suffering was great. The love he had for us all, for this he did not want to leave, for he knew he was breaking our hearts. But he longed to go back to the Father and in some respects he was relieved that his mission was near completion. In each moment of his suffering and abuse he felt the suffering of all humanity.

He felt this completely, in a universal way.

The angels surrounded him and comforted him and at times he transcended the pain and glimpsed heaven.

He was moving between both worlds.

As he lived and died, he wants you to understand that you too are never alone. This is the way we survive what we feel can surely kill us, all of it, no matter the circumstance.

Remember now, in these moments, that all worldly things may be transcended for he has shown the ultimate transcendence, the Resurrection, the proof of everlasting life.

Think of this now, not as a story or a myth.

Call on your soul's remembrance.

For this is surely within you to remember.

The Heart of Love

Feel the power of these words for I speak for him in telling you these things. And firsthand and by his side I witnessed all that I say to you.

Let your hearts open to the understanding of the magnitude of his life, death and Resurrection.

For it is your life.

The Crucifixion

The Heart of Love

The women were there every step of the way
we agonized, we cried out, we fell to our knees
the men were gone
fear had overtaken them

I can only speak for myself when I say
I had no fear
not for me
the unbearable witnessing
of such things done to him
you could only be with him
of him

each step was mine
each time he stumbled
the weight of the cross
the taunts
it was a mob scene

I saw nothing but him
I felt I would not live through it
such was the overwhelming feeling
of being one with him

and even in this
I know it was a comfort to him
for he could feel my agony
and he could feel my infinite love

The Heart of Love

so I walked this way of the cross
and I tell you in complete truth
I hung with him on that cross
and on that day I was aware
of somehow relieving him
in ever the smallest way

for I absorbed his sorrow and I felt his pain
and with all my heart and soul sent him
the radiant burning love
that was transforming within my heart

and this he felt
and this he understood

it is impossible to make known the bitter gall
of that most sorrowful day

for there are no words to describe
the depth of his physical suffering

and the agony and beauty of being witness
to his magnificent forgiving heart

only the glory of his Resurrection
could ever ease the pain
for it would take something so miraculous and divine
to fill your heart with light and love once again

The Heart of Love

it was an honor and a blessing
to stand with the women
the ones who saw nothing
but the truth of heaven before their eyes

and we lifted him with our prayers
and we sustained him with our love
and it was our faces he did see
in these most brutal and terrible moments

and the power of unspeakable acts
and the glorious message of forgiveness
burned in our hearts all the days of our lives

may this message come alive in your hearts
and may his life be testimony
of heaven and of earth

"Truly I tell you, wherever the gospel is preached throughout the world, what she has done will also be told, in memory of her."

Mark 14:9

The Anointing

The Heart of Love

Mary and I delicately, gently and lovingly anointed him at
the tomb
we stroked his hair and kissed his lips
we layed our hands upon his hands
we were ever consciously trying to imprint all of him
into our being
it was purposeful and natural
we worked in silence and unison
our hearts united with love's pure intention

we did not know what to expect
we could only be in the moment
cherishing this final hour
our unbridled grief, mixed with exhausting relief
that his time had come and his suffering ended

but oh how we did not understand
how would our suffering now ever end?
we could not think for we still had him before us
and we honored him in every possible way

with our hearts and our hands we worked our spiritual magic
and I feel in those moments something there took place
for he had transmitted the greatest love and power
to the two Mary's whose love was everlasting
and this it should be known
the importance of these two energies
mother and lover who stood side by side

The Heart of Love

for this was so necessary for one such as he
the love of his mother and the love of his wife
this is what all still yearn for
this is what the Marys provide

call to them when you feel abandoned
call to them when you do not feel loved
for they are ever with you and they shall always guide you
and nothing on earth can cease this loving transmission

understand now, this has been lost
the powerful memory
of the love of these two women
for this Christ needed for his life here on earth
and this filled his heart as he walked upon this earth

now we must fill our hearts with their message
now we must fill our hearts with divine feminine love
so gently and softly they held him, loved and comforted him
they offer this to you for you yearn for this love

look all around you to those who carry this light
for it is surely there and you may surely feel it
follow your hearts to the beautiful divine mother
the mother of all, your light and protector

feel the love of Mary our mother
and grace yourselves with the love of Mary Magdalene
for these are vibrations of everlasting love
these are vibrations from heaven most high

The Heart of Love

as Mary Magdalene begins to be acknowledged
for the feminine love she was destined to give
she takes her place with our most beloved mother
they are hand in hand in offering you their love

for as these things were suppressed through the ages
so has love been suppressed here on earth
long do you search for the love of these Marys
long do you ache to be held once again

as falsehoods fall away in all dimensions
the falsehoods of your lives will fall away as well
for this is a new day
the day of truth and divine love
and all is being restored
for love and peace shall reign

see the beloved Marys standing now before you
see their arms outstretched to welcome you home
for the divine feminine will fill you and heal you
and your memories of love will be born once again

Resurrection

The Heart of Love

This is beyond words
for what took place was not of this world
this is why it was so difficult to comprehend for many
they believed it but how could it be?

after the agony of that day we were completely worn out
physically and emotionally
all that kept us going was the thought of still caring for him
for at least we had his physical body
to still gaze upon and touch

I could not wait to lay my eyes upon him and anoint him
for I felt at least
he was out of their hands and into mine

I could think of nothing else
seeing him and honoring him
and most of all, saying farewell

how can I describe how my heart was breaking

I was not prepared for the sight of the empty tomb

oh how much more unbearable can this become?
they have taken him even in death
taken him from me
in how many ways must they insult him and defile him?
inconceivable it was
my heart froze with terror and longing
I felt I would collapse
no, I could not bear it!

The Heart of Love

where have they taken him?

and what happened next was so heavenly and miraculous
it is what I lived on all the rest of my days

for he had come to comfort me and truly allow me
to glimpse heaven firsthand
and this I did

and I was filled once again with the holy spirit
and I was filled with the power and transforming energy
of God in all His glory
through my beloved
for he appeared to me
through the power and majesty of heaven

and this was such an experience, I was, as if,
not even myself
I was transfixed and immediately taken
from the heartbreak and tragic grief
of the moment before
and lifted and filled
with heaven itself

understand these things are true
for I was there and I was witness
and just as these things happened to me
this is now happening to you
for you are hearing these words

The Heart of Love

open your hearts and feel the truth
and infinite wonder
of all that is being put before you
for if you are hearing these words
you too will be transfixed and transformed
and will allow yourselves to glimpse heaven

know he is with you
as he came to me on that day
I come to you now
with this message of hope
and this message of love

for all is not what it seems
and this I give you
as he gave this to me

may you open your hearts
to the transforming love of Christ

The Heart of Love

Belonging to no one
he gave himself to the world

seeking nothing
he gave all

owning nothing
he possessed all that matters

the light of love shining forth
touching all

words of truth
vibrating into the hearts of man

living in complete divinity
but feeling everything as a man

demonstrating the possibility
of human enlightenment

curing them of their ills
filling them with hope
restoring faith

walking the land
in the complete embodiment
of his mission

The Heart of Love

rising above pain
and fear
jealousy and hatred

gracefully extending his beautiful smile
deeply caring and weeping for those he loved

he was a man living in total divinity

he was and is the inspiration

and connection

for all time

his story goes on

it is written and spoken

but more than this

it is the feeling deep in your hearts
the feeling of love so overpowering
you feel you may die if you truly allow it

this is the power and the glory of the one called Jesus

"Do not weep or grieve or be in doubt, for his grace will be with you all and will protect you. Rather let us praise his greatness, for he has prepared us and made us truly human."

The Gospel of Mary Magdalene

After

The Heart of Love

After his death I continued with all I had been doing when he was here but everything had now changed. For once he was gone there was still a lot of fear and struggle and arguments over what should be done. There was nothing to be decided, it was so simple. It was not about rules and position.

I was broken hearted beyond what I thought I could bear and the sorrow of what I had witnessed, what had been done to him, did torment me still. Even the glory of the Resurrection did not ease the pain of missing him in the physical world.

But I was ever transformed by all that had transpired and I knew I would continue for what else was there? I had been given a gift, through my beloved and never would I turn away and never would I forget. For all the days of my life were spent living the truth of why he had come and why I had been blessed to be his beloved.

If all would only consider the simplicity of his life and live in peace and harmony with one another and with nature. Why have you forgotten? Why must beliefs and rules take precedence over the heart and the spirit? Let all these notions now fall away. Look into the eyes of another, for there you shall see him and there you shall see yourself.

This is all you need to understand.

Wake up to the feeling of love long buried.

Reach for the stars and heaven.

Look up not away.

Let yourselves feel all it means to be alive.

Let yourselves remember the truest and kindest words ever spoken.

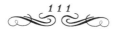

The Heart of Love

Allow yourselves the gift of living with all that is heavenly
all that has been given
for he has been remembered
and you may forget and turn away
but his words will continue to be spoken
and his heart will continue to love
for it is eternal and everlasting...

Meditation
of the
Sacred Heart

The Heart of Love

All that is heartfelt is connected to him
for he is the most sacred heart
consciously connect your heart to his
you may do this with the breath

you may imagine your heart radiating out
and entering his
and his radiating out to yours

this is truly the exchange that is always taking place
you may magnify this
by consciously putting your attention there

surround yourself with the light of the Resurrection
for feeling this light and vibration
will help in your transcending

for there is no time
and you may directly connect
into that most powerful energy
and feel the power in the transforming light
of the Resurrection

this is meant for you
these are the ways in which you should spend your time
in contemplation and direct participation
for the light of Christ is available to you

The Heart of Love

as you seek it you shall be it

as you understand more and more
the power in these intentions
you will grow in love
and you will cleanse
and illuminate your energy field
with the love of Christ

this is why he lived
and this is why he died

accept and know
that all these things are meant for you
and now is the time to enter the silence
and remember
for his love is infinite and eternal
and he joins you
and is happy to fill you
with this gift of remembrance

Divine Union

The Heart of Love

Oh divine union
oh holy night
oh the stars in heaven
and the earth beneath our feet
hand in hand
electrified by love

two hearts beating
in perfect unison

world out of balance
world forged by men

this union
gifted to one another
and presented to all who had eyes to see
meant to be known
throughout the ages
to unify and glorify
the truth of man and woman

we whispered our love
we cried out our agony
we dared to be
the living, breathing truth of God
God within
pure, loving, eternal
brilliant and natural
as the sea, the sky, the earth

The Heart of Love

oh dusty days
and long internments
walking, speaking, touching, healing
living the golden way
expressing this divine energy to all
releasing it out into the cosmos
to merge with all that is seen
and all that is unseen

to remain as a sacred healing balm
for all the world

for it is always shining there

for we understood that this was to be done
we understood that the day would come
when the memory of this glorious union
would be remembered
by the beloveds

and as was done then
the spell of forgetting would be broken
and eyes would widen with wonder
and miracles would come
and love would burst forth
for the truest memory of love
is everywhere
and within everyone

we were guided by a power
a power that connected us to one another
and to every man, woman and child
all felt this in our presence

many were frightened as they continue to be today

what is this fear of the power of love?

The Heart of Love

what is the renouncing in the equality in all that is love?

these fears are the fears of old
these energies continue to confuse
to nullify the truth

the truth lies within you
the truth is the guardian of the most holy

there is much more to be revealed
and the earth shall quake and the heavens shall roar

for the awakening must come
and love and truth shall reign

quietly go within
feel every truth
for these acknowledgments are the jewels
along the golden path
the pathway to peace and enlightenment
do not look for greater truths
until you have turned to your own

for one truth resonates with another

and the energies gather
until the magnitude of the greatest truth of all
is felt and lived

you gather as we once did
you speak of these things
and you remember somewhere in your heart
the wonder and beauty of the paradise we brought to earth
our divine vow
our loving demonstration

The Heart of Love

love is beautiful
love does not hurt
love rejoices for one another
love is kind
love is the force behind all that manifests
in goodness and light

how do you live with a loving heart in a world of madness
and anger and doubt?

through the light of Christ and the heart of Mary Magdalene

for he and I lived this love

through unbearable trials

and I say to you it can be done
and I say to you it must be done

for if you have ears to hear
and eyes to see
to accept these words
you have the heart to know
the truth of all that is being brought forth

it does not take courage to do these things
it takes only love
for love is your natural state of being
and love is the creator of all there is

gaze at the stars
and you shall feel love
swim in the sea and you shall feel love
walk upon the earth and you shall feel love
look into another's eyes
and truly know love

The Heart of Love

I come at this time and place
I speak through her my beloved counterpart
for she has allowed this memory so true
only fear prevents the remembering
only love can bring you back home

home is the truth
and the truth is the light
the light of love
in each and every heart

look to one another
touch one another
hold one another
in your wondrous embrace

draw the light of heaven down through your head
pull the love of the earth up through your feet
feel these energies merge in the heart
and release out through your hands
the healing power of love

this is as it was
and this it shall be

truth

remembrance

love

All
Divine Unions

The Heart of Love

The energies are rising. We must merge with these energies, encouraging the masculine to embrace and awaken to their own Christ light and Mary Magdalene within.

How is this done?

Speaking, for gradually the suppression shall be cleared away and the vibrations of the true voice shall be heard and remembered. For those who do not wish to remember, it is their choice but the time is at hand and the opportunity ever present.

Shall you enter the vibration with full understanding, faith and remembrance? You know in your hearts the truth of the message. You feel in your souls the growing, the urgent call to act upon your deepest feelings. These feelings are the beginnings of remembrance for the forgetting has been strong and many have grown comfortable with only what they see and hear with their earthly senses. We ask you to go beyond this world and as you, the feminine aspect of God, move into the power and truth of your being, you shall create an opening for the masculine to follow.

The time is at hand. Even now some of you are thinking, I have not known this exchange, we speak another language than that of the masculine. And this is truly how it feels but I say to you that I have lived, and I say to you that I have known the extraordinary beauty of a love that transcends all thought and all that is brought forth by the mind.

For the soul is the heart of the memory of love and the mind is the anesthetic that leads to the forgetting.

The Heart of Love

For love is where you come from and love is where you shall return.

Begin now to feel this most powerful remembrance. Begin now to vow to open your heart and your soul by quieting the mind for this is the new dawning and you are the living prophecy of love.

You are the women come in this time and place to transcend all, to release this infinite power, to use all you have to awaken, your eyes, your ears, your voice and most of all your heart. For I am with you and the silence must come to end. I am speaking now for at this time there are those who have awakened to believe all that is being brought forth. You are among them. You are chosen and you have chosen.

Let us begin to merge our collective energies

Let us step into the power, the beauty, the heart of all there is.

And let it be known and let it be heard that those who have chosen to merge with like kind, woman to woman and man to man have heard and felt the call to be and absorb, to merge and unite with the purest energies of love. You have chosen to expand and accelerate such loving unions. You have chosen to transcend all worldly boundaries, to live in the truth of you heart's burning desire.

We wish you to acknowledge your beauty and to move into the spirit of these most blessed unions. For woman to woman you continue to send out powerful feminine vibrations meant to heal all of humanity and the planet. And man to man you celebrate the feminine aspect of God within yourselves and this aids the world in ways you can not comprehend.

The Heart of Love

So let us unite in love.

Let us acknowledge every aspect of love and let us acknowledge the truth of love, that each loving union is blessed and sacred. Each loving union answers the call, the call to truth, the call to enlightenment and the powerful emergence of the divine within each and every being.

All divine partnerships must now come out of the shadows and stand for love. For fear and denial have created the forgetting and the memory of love shall shake these untruths.

We shall rise in love.
We shall embrace our power.
We shall lead the way.

I stand with you and for you.

And I say to you, the miraculous begins here and now.
This voice is being used for the purpose of awakening the many.
It is golden and divine.

Use your voices as she has chosen to use hers. Have courage, have heart and know that we the women shall bring the feminine energy back into the world, back into the hearts of all mankind and this shall be the true awakening and this shall be the light of Christ reborn.
And this shall be the truth.

The Heart of Love

The equal partnership

The divine union

Masculine and feminine

Christ and Magdalene

He steps aside as he did then, encouraging all to be seen and heard. For he, the one who is so loved, asks you now to come forward, beseeches you to trust your own heart.

He stands behind each and every one of you
arms outstretched
palms raised towards you
and says unto you
go forward beloveds
take the hand of Mary Magdalene
as I have done
for she is as you
and your heart is hers.

"But when he, the spirit of the truth, comes, he will guide you in to all the truth. He will not speak on his own; he will speak only what he hears, and he will tell you what is to come."

John 16:13

The Heart of Love

What is the soul
the everlasting spirit
given with love
to enlighten and heal
for what more do we need
than to nourish it
and honor it
what more should we know
than we shall not forsake it
what is the soul
our shining companion
of eternal truth
and memory of home
how shall we remember
it's deep abiding message
and where shall we turn
if not to its blessing

The Truth

The Heart of Love

It was not my intention when I committed to writing this book that I would reveal the whole truth of what transpired. I was afraid. It has taken me several years to absorb and understand what has happened to me. When the divine comes calling you can never be prepared because we are so ingrained in the world and these experiences are not of the world.

I have never doubted the miraculous blessing that has come to me but I doubted myself. I worried that I did not have what it takes to come out and be all I was meant to be in the world. I have made my way through this experience slowly though those around me have encouraged me and supported me and nudged me lovingly forward.

Most of the time I have yearned to be in a monastery or some quiet place where I could do nothing but write. This is where the merging of heaven and earth takes place because the miraculous is unfolding in the midst of our ordinary lives.

I believe something wonderful is happening in our world and I am so thankful that I came into the world with a spark of remembrance of where I came from. When the spark is ignited and begins to burn in your heart there is no turning back. The flame begins to burn ever brighter and the light of this flame illuminates the truth.

As we step out one by one, the power of the truth shall change our world. We must see the truth, feel the truth, speak the truth and be the truth. I have been blessed and encouraged by those I have met who have stepped out fully into their own truth. I wish to be among them.

What follows is my past life regression. It shines the light on what was revealed to me during my vision of Jerusalem. There is much I have learned since that day. Many of us on earth today are carrying vibrations of the people and times of the time of Christ. These memories and

vibrations are awakening in souls all across the planet. I believe these sparks of remembrance are within us all.

I have made my way through this incredible journey comforted and encouraged by the many people I have met who share these memories. Many of us have sought help in understanding the meaning in these extraordinary experiences. One of the paths of discovery has been through past life regression work. This is a powerful tool to unlock emotions and memories we all carry throughout our lifetimes. It has been an enlightening and healing method for us all.

The soul sparks of Mary Magdalene and others are coming forth through many people to help awaken us and to heal us. I did not intend to include my regression because there did not seem to be a way to explain the infinite cosmic relationship revealed here. I have only come to understand that these sparks are within us all and certain times, events or people may jolt us into remembering.

We are all divinely connected. We are all on a path of spiritual discovery and we are all being aided by many spiritual beings. I offer you my story so that it may merge with your own story, so that we may all consciously divinely connect with one another and with all the Beloveds who have so graciously come forward.

I continue to be inspired by those who have come forth to speak and live in the truth of these magnificent energies of 2,000 years ago. All that was seeded at that time comes forth now to unite us in truth, love, peace and oneness. I wish to do my part in helping to ignite this memory, for there are those of you who will read this and the spark in your heart will ignite and you will remember, for one truth leads to another. It is my hope and prayer that as we continue to encourage one another we will begin to unite and live in the one most magnificent and universal truth of all.

Be not afraid
for all wonders and majesty
are yours to create
do not think it is beyond the veil
for the treasure lies within
and is only sleeping

The Heart of Love

Passages through time
gathering wisdom
falling asleep
only to be awakened
carrying memories
from times long past
ride the vibrations
of the new and shining dawning
hear the sweet whispers
calling your true name
open to worlds
you thought far away
follow your heart
for it will surely lead you
down the path of your dreams
where your destiny awaits you

Journey to Jerusalem

Past Life Regression with Julia Ingram,

author of <u>The Lost Sisterhood, The Return of Mary Magdalene, the Mother Mary and Other Holy Women</u>

Julia   What do you see?

Gail   I am standing next to him, holding his hand.

Julia   Feel his hand, which hand is his hand in?

Gail   My left, holding his right.

Julia   Look at your hand, look at his, it's alright to see.

Gail   (weeping) even that much is....it's like the perfection of those two hands....it's what everyone is still looking for and just as people carry the crucifixion in their hearts, they also still carry that memory of that perfect love and that is why everyone is still searching and always disappointed that they can't seem to find that feeling.

Julia   With another person?

Gail   Well they think it's with another person.

Julia   And what else is going on?

Gail   (weeping) We're just talking.

Julia   About?

Gail   Everything, just like a regular day, just walking and talking and sharing everything. I don't feel any anguish in this day. There is no one around. There is no pressure. The crowds are not around. We're just by ourselves.

Julia   Anything else to remember about this regular day?

Gail   He's showing me something. I feel like he is touching my third eye with his index finger.

Julia   What happens when he does that?

Gail   He's talking to me about it, about seeing.

Julia   And you're weeping because?

Gail   Because of all the things to see....I think I'm seeing this because I have been afraid to see and they are showing me this particular thing because they want me to know that he wants me to see.

Julia   Keep going.

Gail   I am very open to it. Then. And I already know these things but he elevates them or encourages you to go beyond anything you already know. And that is what he did about everything. That's what he tried to do. And he is very happy because I am so open and this gives him great joy.

Julia   The teacher is always thrilled when the pupil gets it, although I

don't think this is quite a teacher - pupil relationship.

Gail   No. It's an equal partnership. I see us still standing there but you know he is a very joyful person, very funny. He loves joking around.

Julia   Is he joking around right now?

Gail   Yes. I feel like I'm standing there but I couldn't really see his face but for a second there I could sort of glimpse that smile but oh......(weeping) it's almost too much to see it! And for a minute there I thought I saw him joking around with his mother.

Julia   Please remember that.

Gail   He's running after her and she is screaming and laughing. I'm just sensing all this love and joy and closeness of the three. (weeping) It is like they are the trinity of some kind.

Julia   Well you have your own relationship with Mary that is very precious.

Gail   She has an understanding of everything. Everything. And an acceptance of everything but that changed later on. She became different. I don't think she ever got it back. But they want her to get it back. And she will. Because you know, the after, just got stuck in our hearts.

The Heart of Love

Julia Just keep focusing in on Mary's direction going forward or backwards to the next significant event.

Gail I see the crowds gathering and he would always be whispering things to me.

Julia Like what?

Gail (laughing) He didn't think they understood what he was saying but he said he had to say it anyway.

Julia What is he saying today?

Gail Love one another. He found it so interesting that they would come and listen but their minds were so carried away. He tried to teach them how to quiet the mind but you know the times were so difficult. People had so much to worry about.

Julia When he's talking to the crowds what are you doing?

Gail I'm touching them. I'm going through the crowd. I'm going through the crowd! And I can tell, Oh my God! I can tell what's wrong with each person...and then I touch them....while he's speaking.

Julia And what do you notice when you touch them?

Gail They feel....transformed. Oh....the men don't like it either.

Julia The men don't like what? That you're participating?

Gail   Yes, the ones around him, some of them. It annoys them.
They don't think a woman should be so obvious!
You should not draw attention to yourself. You should keep quiet
and this is too much of a display and doing the kinds of things that he
would do. They were more confused in general....about everything.
I was not confused, at all.

It was natural to me, natural, like I was born knowing and then he just
became part of it and I loved it...I loved it... touching the people and this
was part of the outward showing of how things should be. And then
while he was speaking, he would just be speaking. I can see myself
moving through that crowd and touching those people.

Julia   So the combination of the word and the touch.

Gail   Exactly! That's it, that's it...that's it....and looking at him. All eyes
would be looking at him, hearing him. I would be called to the ones who
needed to be physically touched.

Julia   Are others moving around in the crowd as well?

Gail   Not on this day.

Julia   Just the two of you on this day.

Gail   Yes. No one else is doing this. I think that's why they are angry.
I don't know whether he told them they couldn't or I don't know.
I am not sure if they were not ready. I think I did this first and
this was a bone of contention.

The Heart of Love

Julia   Who is most jealous?

Gail   Peter and James.

Julia   Who are you feeling the most support from?

Gail   Mary, his mother.

Julia   Any of the men?

Gail   I don't know.

Julia   Move forward now to the next significant event.

Gail   They're taking him away. I am sensing a lot of chaos, people running around, beside themselves, almost insane, insane, like just going insane. They took him and everyone is insane. That's what it feels like.

Julia   Where you there when they took him or is someone telling you?

Gail   I saw that but I don't think I was there.

Julia   What happens next?

Gail   Oh Mary! Oh! She doesn't accept it (sobbing) she thinks they are going to let him go! She can't cope with it! She keeps telling herself that they are going to let him go.

Julia   Do you have any of that hope yourself?

Gail   None. She cannot go there. She cannot. She thinks something will happen. She cannot bear it. And I am comforting her because it is almost worse that she can't.... (sobbing)....and he didn't really talk to her about it before or prepare her because he couldn't bear it but he prepared me all the time so it was different.... even though it was terrible.

Julia   He didn't talk to her about it before?

Gail   Not like he did with me. Not like he did with me because he would say something, refer to it, if necessary but he was not able to emotionally take her any further into it because of the look on her face. He couldn't do it (sobbing). But we were together so much and alone a lot so....and I was so always wanting to know everything. She knew; it's not that she didn't know but she went into some kind of a state (sobbing) of denial. She couldn't face it when it came. Oh God. And this was a.... my God, never mind the circumstance but to have to watch one another suffer from it, oh my God. It's unbearable.

Julia   Mary's suffering is unbearable to you?

Gail   Completely. It still is. It still is.

Julia   What happens next?

Gail   Oh...Oh...my God.

Julia   Where are you now?

Gail   Standing again with him and my God, I am seeing such a thing! Sometimes we would be standing there and we could actually see the rays of light coming down onto us both. We could see it. That was something. We could see it, feel it.

The Heart of Love

Julia   It didn't happen all the time? There were occasions when this would happen?

Gail   Yes and it would sustain us, just bring you back into the knowing of the power of everything and that it was bigger than the two of us even.... bigger. It was like they were showering us with all kinds of... everything would come down in that, strength and wisdom and everything and it would generate us to go on with the bigger picture. It was necessary.

Julia   You said they were showering us. Who are they?

Gail   All the Heavenly beings; all the spiritual beings who are always surrounding us...it happens....people just don't, it happens all the time.

Julia   You just see it.

Gail   Yes. But it is also exceptionally exceptional (laughing) because of the magnitude of the mission.

Julia   I imagine Gail has experienced spirit.

Gail   Well, I just saw, that is what they call, because they must call it something, the Holy Spirit, and I did see that image of the dove above us and that we were very connected to that.... (whispering) to the dove. That is why they showed me that symbol, messenger of hope and peace and love, unity and enlightenment....and freedom, flight.... everything. Somebody just said, I heard this before but I just heard it now, I don't know why "Mary Keeper of The Doves." What is that? I don't know.

Julia   Access the part of you that does know.

Gail   I don't know.

Julia   Then you'll know later.

The Heart of Love

Julia Move forward or backward. What else?

Gail I was just getting a sense of the teaching that I would do with the women.

Julia Please go to an occasion when you were meeting with the women.

Gail I was always telling them that they were more than their husbands, trying to wake them up. They are so scared. Scared of their own husbands and I am so annoyed because it is so unnatural, to me, and I try to remind them that it is unnatural to them. If they could just feel their own feelings and not what is going on around them. There is something crazy going on.....backwards.....and then I try to teach them the same thing I always try to teach everyone today.

Julia If there is just one thing you could teach them what would you want them to get?

Gail That although it shouldn't necessarily have to be this way it is essential for the woman to be the spiritual advisor to the husband. If they are choosing to be in a marriage, this is an essential part of the feminine because the masculine suppresses these things and lives in the mind and the third dimension and the feminine naturally does not. And if you want to have a chance of an equal partnership you have to be the light that ignites the spark of memory in the masculine because it is there, they just forgot it.

And it can be done. And it should be done...with love from the very beginning. And also mother to child, mother to son especially. This is a very, very important role of the feminine...to awaken the spirituality of their sons, anyone they come in contact with of the masculine gender, brother, whatever.

And be happy that you have this gift and be loving in sharing it and patient. Once you offer and offer and if you see a response, if you see even a tiny step forward than you know that there is hope, that they wish to see and they wish to know.

Some do not wish to see and know. Then you have to decide how long you will put yourself into it. You must use your intuition and when you have done all you can then that relationship must end because you must fully be everything you were born to be and it doesn't matter what times you live in, it doesn't matter. You have to be. And it doesn't matter the outcome. It doesn't matter what will happen to you because of it. You have to speak and fully be who you are.

That's it. That's it. And that is what, that is the essence of Mary Magdalene. That is it. And I feel I was born remembering that because I have been doing it my whole life in this life and I know I was born remembering it. And I love that.... I love that. And I love women. And I love men who love women but I love men who love women as real women. I love that. There's nothing like women. It's just the truth.

Julia   So in this gathering that you are looking at today. Is anyone getting it, even a little bit?

Gail   Oh yes. They get it. They feel it but they are so terrified. It's still going on today, oh my God. They're terrified. They're just too terrified. So I am trying to move them more into their own heart of remembrance. But that's all you can do. That's all you can do.

It is the same thing me with them as them and their marriages. You can do, say, be and you can't force anybody to open. Some are not going to open in whatever life it is. They are not going to do it. They have choice and you have to accept that some people are not going to come along. They're just not, and they're not supposed to, for whatever reason.

But you know when you begin to resonate your true divinity, that's what you attract and that's how you vibrate and many will fall away

from your life...not out of judgment but you attract those of like heart, not mind but heart.

And I feel that that is where I am now, surrounded by like hearts, fulfilling each other, sustaining one another. I feel we have brought that heaven to earth in our memories and our willingness to be who we are.....here and now.

Julia   Beautiful, thank you.

Gail   You're welcome. I wish there was a pill I could give to the women. (laughter).

Julia   Could you recall a time when you were younger and you were learning from Mother Mary. I know she was one of your teachers.

Gail   Oh we are drawing something in the dirt. She and I, she's at one end and I'm at the other and we're making some kind of a design in the earth. It seems to be like an octagon kind of shape and then we're putting little stones at each point. In the middle there is a circle. You stand in the circle.

Julia   What happens when you stand in the circle?

Gail   I think it's about remembering. I think you get information. We are creating a power place, like the Native Americans do but we were doing it then.

Julia   Memorize the shape and the stones. I think you are going to be using this.

Gail   It's funny because it does have a Native American feel to it. I think they did this exact same thing. I had a very significant Native American life. I feel like I did this again then because it's more like a spider web outline. I feel like I am going to see this somewhere. They are still using this. In the Native American life we used feathers and I am getting a duality, a connection from that to that.

Julia   Let's recall another time when perhaps even after Yeshua's death, when Mary was still working with people, still healing.

Gail   You know I always thought that after, she was always so heartbroken but she went on, but I'm just getting now that that wasn't it.

Julia   Now what are you getting?

Gail   I'm getting that she really, really, really understood every bit of it and that she loved her work all through her life, that she....it's just so strange because I don't feel....here I feel that I have been carrying this sadness but feeling her after.... I'm feeling much more of her completeness, her completeness within herself, that nothing could take that away and that she was just very complete and very.....not taking away the trauma of that and she carried it of course but she was complete unto herself. That's the other thing. That is the other thing that she wishes to convey. Be complete unto yourself no matter what. No matter what.

Julia   Where does your source of strength come from Mary?

Gail   From those rays of light. Those rays of light come from above and they exist within you and they merge and you should always be aware and thankful, ever thankful, because that is the glory of heaven and that is your heaven on earth and it is a speck of what is to come and what we are going to experience. And that is where she is and that is where he is. That is where all the spiritual beings are and they are always emanating and always around us helping us and encouraging us and adoring us.... adoring us. And the more you think about that and the more you allow yourself to feel that, the more you can remember who you are and live your life accordingly.

The Heart of Love

Julia   There are a lot of different opinions on where Mary went after Yeshua's death. Do you have any interest in looking at that?

Gail   Yes I do. Well I can only say this, I feel very compelled to go to France in this life for whatever reason. I feel that she was in France.

Julia   So focus in on that feeling and ask the Magdalene to show you. You may have gone several places. So let yourself be surprised by what you see and hear.

Gail   I just saw a little hill. I just see a little hillside that was very special to her.

Julia   Special because?

Gail   Oh God, I don't know. Oh when I was a kid there was a hill. I called it my hill. They just showed me that. That's why I loved that hill. It was a memory of that hill.

Julia   What was special about that hill back then?

Gail   It was where I went for quiet contemplation. Ohhhh....oh my God I'm getting something strange here....(deep sigh).... well I would go to this hill to meet with him, after. This is why I was perceiving that the suffering wasn't as I think of it somehow because she was still with him, still with him. Now I'm getting that this is why it is very important for people to understand that the soul lives on and that they are always with you. It's not just a hocus pocus parlor game. It is very, very healing. I'm going into another world...

Julia   And what is in this other world?

Gail   I don't see anything it is just this feeling...wow. Something is going on here isn't it?

Julia   Yes

The Heart of Love

Gail   (deep breath and a most transcendent experience that cannot be explained in words)

Julia   Can you put any of this into words?

Gail   I feel that a healing took place. Could you sense who was here?

Julia   I sensed several, Yeshua, Michael. Yes and light coming into you and going out of you.

Gail   My whole body. It was so strong.

Julia   What was healed?

Gail   I hope the fear of seeing. I hope.

Julia   Is that what was healed?

Gail   Well I want to say my heart.

Julia   That's a lot.

Gail   Yes.

The Heart of Love

Those who came before us
those who stand beside us
those who live within us
who comfort, love and guide us

those whose lives have shown
the endless possibilities
of love and truth and peace
and life so everlasting

those who live within our hearts
when desperate and alone
those who live within our words
when truth is bravely spoken

those who help to carry us
when fallen and forsaken
those who's every breath upon this earth
has given meaning

to every thought and every word
and every prayer in action
to show that every heart and mind
are blessings sent from heaven
and every opportunity
a sacred undertaking

and as they came before us
and as they stand beside us
and as they dwell within us
that we shall ever know

the beauty of their resonance
their faith throughout all time
their everlasting presence
and the stories of their lives

The Heart of Love

Amazing grace
fill me and save me
from all of my doubts
and all of my fears
from all my cautions
and all my misgivings
from all that holds me
in bondage here

amazing grace
open my heart
and help me to feel
the light within
lift me and guide me
strengthen and find me
comfort me now
in my yearning for home

amazing grace
carry me forward
illuminate all
so I may reveal
my soul and calling
and my true longing
my desire to be
pure grace unfolding

The Heart of Love

Whosoever shall open their hearts
whosoever shall answer the call
shall be the consecrated, born in to new life
a life of love remembered and renewed
a life of living a true heaven on earth

the path is now clear
the way showers now stepping forward
in truth, honor and filled with the memory
and love of all of heaven

you come forward one by one
you move forward step by step
you participate in the initiation once more
and by your vow to live in honor
of the truth, the way, and the light
you ready yourselves
for the dawning of the new world
the world you dream
the world you have chosen to create
by thought word and deed

you are the peacemakers
therefore be peace
you are the way showers
therefore shine the light

for the light of Christ lives within your hearts
and the truth of Mary Magdalene awakens your souls
divine symbols of unity, equality, love and peace

go forth in remembrance
of the power and the beauty
in this most sacred and perfect balance
for within you lies the dream
awakened . . .

"The breath and soul of the feminine now breathed back into being, and upon the wings of the wind, is carried far and wide. It is infinite in its breath and divine in its healing power."
-Mary Magdalene

CPSIA information can be obtained
at www.ICGtesting.com
Printed in the USA
BVHW031306230721
612726BV00009B/35